Gratitude Journal

A DAILY 5 MINUTE GUIDE

FOR MEDITATION

REFLECTION AND SELF CARE

This Journal Belongs To

_____

_____

Gratitude Jar

A gratitude jar is a delightful Thanksgiving tradition that can be done individually or the whole family may participate in it.

A gratitude jar works by writing down something you're grateful for on a piece of paper and putting it in the jar. Then, on Thanksgiving, take out the paper slips and read them aloud.

EXAMPLES:

1. "I am grateful for my cat because she makes me laugh."
2. "I am thankful for the dinner I had tonight. It was my favorite: pizza!"
3. "I appreciate my grandma because she visited me when I was sick."

This simple act allows people to focus on the positive aspects of their lives. You'll notice that as you individually jot down things for which you're grateful, you'll feel and recognize appreciation more frequently. This "gratitude game" also encourages happier and more grateful attitudes at home.

Our brains' helpful tendency, on the other hand, tends to focus on the less-than-fun aspects of our lives, preventing us from recalling all the good times. Here's where the thankfulness jar comes in handy!

Make the ideal gratitude jar

You might start your appreciation game by making your own gratitude jar. Here's how to do it:

- Begin with a clean, lidded jar. Any container will suffice, but a Mason jar is ideal.
- To label your jar, use the free printable.
- The thanks card printable can be printed out.

This is where you'll jot down the things for which you're grateful..

- Make it uniquely yours! Kids will enjoy using stickers, paint, and other craft supplies to decorate your appreciation jar.

How to Make the Most of a Gratitude Jar

Your family can approach your thankfulness jar in a variety of ways. Here are a few suggestions:

- Allow your children to jot down something they're grateful for that occurred during the day as part of their goodnight routine.
- Keep your gratitude jar, slips of paper, and pens or pencils handy and jot down things you're thankful for throughout the day.
- Make it a Thanksgiving Day exercise for your visitors by asking them to jot down one thing for which they are grateful.

- Place the jar and pieces of paper in a high-traffic area where you'll see them often, such as your kitchen counter,
- bathroom vanity, or laundry room. Make it a daily aim to jot down one item you're grateful for and place it in your thankfulness jar.

Gratitude Jar journaling:

A gratitude jar journal is a book that keeps track of the things for which you are grateful. Individuals who want to focus their attention on the positive aspects of their lives utilize gratitude notebooks. In the subject of positive psychology, gratitude, or the sense of appreciation or thanks, has gotten a lot of attention.

Gratitude is a virtue that we should cultivate. Gratitude must be planted, watered, clothed, and harvested throughout the Believer.

Gratitude encapsulates the essence of being created, finite, fallen, forgiven, and sustained by the God of all kindness.

Throughout the Bible, believers are reminded of the significance of being thanks and expressing thankfulness on a regular basis. However, living a grateful life isn't easy. It takes time, effort, and consistent.

According to research, thankfulness cannot be lumped in with other emotions such as happiness or rage because, unlike other emotions, gratitude requires intentional effort. That is, in order to be appreciative, we must first acknowledge that something has been done for our benefit.

Gratitude Journal

A gratitude journal is a book that keeps track of the things for which you are grateful. Individuals who want to focus their attention on the positive aspects of their lives utilize gratitude notebooks. In the subject of positive psychology, gratitude, or the sense of appreciation or thanks, has gotten a lot of attention.

Examples:

- "I am grateful for my cat because she makes me laugh."
- "I am glad that I wake up daily, and spending the whole day in fresh air around the nature
- "I appreciate my grandma because she visited me when I was sick."

Gratitude is a virtue that we should cultivate. Gratitude must be planted, watered, clothed, and harvested throughout the Believer.

Gratitude encapsulates the essence of being created, finite, fallen, forgiven, and sustained by the God of all kindness.

Throughout the Bible, believers are reminded of the significance of being happy with what their God has bestowed upon them on a regular basis. However, living a grateful life isn't easy. It takes time, effort, and consistent.

Psychologists who study moral formation have spent a lot of time attempting to figure out what the benefits of being satisfied with life are and how to get people to feel more grateful. This study, when combined with Scripture, provides some key insights and suggestions about how we can more successfully use gratitude practices as a spiritual discipline.

According to research, being relieved cannot be lumped in with other emotions such as happiness or rage because, unlike other emotions, gratitude requires intentional effort. That is, in order to be appreciative, we must first acknowledge that something has been done for our benefit

Benefits:

You could find it difficult to get started with your journaling, especially if you've never kept one before.

Reminding yourself of the benefits of thankfulness on a daily basis can give you the motivation you need to keep going.

Consider writing down some of these advantages and posting them in your journal or on your refrigerator as a reminder:

- Writing down about Gratitude has been shown to boost long-term happiness by 10% and reduce depression by 30%.

- It can help you feel better physically, resulting in less aches and pains.
- It can help you sleep better and for longer periods of time.
- It can help you create new friendships and improve your relationships.

Start small:

We all go through terrible times, and finding the positives might be difficult when you're down. The benefit of maintaining a thankfulness diary is that it causes you to consider what you have to be grateful for. It doesn't even have to be a big deal!

Begin by observing your immediate surroundings. Perhaps you should be thankful for the pen in your hand because it allows you to jot down your ideas. Perhaps you should be thankful that your house has power, which allows you to see the page you're writing on. You may be thankful for the warm, comfortable bed in which you sleep each night. It could also be thankfulness for a good who texted you earlier in the day.

Begin by observing your immediate surroundings. Perhaps you should be thankful for the pen in your hand because it allows you to jot down your ideas. Perhaps you should be thankful that your house has power, which allows you to see the page you're writing on. You may be thankful for the warm, comfortable bed in which you sleep each night. It could also be thankfulness for a good who texted you earlier in the day.

Get Specific:

Rather than simply writing, "I'm grateful for my bed," try to be more specific in your gratitude diary.

Explain why you're grateful for it in detail. 'I'm grateful for my bed since it's a safe and comfortable place where I can relax and rest every night,' for example. 'I'm glad for my friend since she complimented my hair earlier and made me feel good about myself,' for example. Knowing why you're thankful can help you receive more from your gratitude notebook. Keeping a thankfulness book is just one of the many fantastic ways you may enhance your mental health by changing your mindset.

Gratitude letter

A letter of thanks, also known as a Gratitude letter, is written when one person or group desires to express gratitude to another. When the addressee is a friend, acquaintance, or relative, personal thank-you letters are sometimes written by hand. These gratitude letters are frequently written in the style of a professional business letter.

Writing a Gratitude letter:

Bring to mind someone who has done something for you that you are grateful for but to whom you have never expressed your gratitude. This could be a family member, a friend, a teacher, or a coworker. Choose someone who is still alive and could meet you in person in the coming week. Selecting a person or behavior that you haven't thought about in a while—something that isn't always on your mind—might be most beneficial.

Steps:

Now, using the instructions below as a guide, compose a letter to one of these persons.

- Write as if you're speaking directly to this person ("Dear ").
- Don't be concerned about your spelling or punctuation.
- Describe what this individual accomplished, why you are grateful to them, and how their actions influenced your life in particular words. Make an effort to be as specific as possible.
- Describe what you're doing right now in your life and how you recall their efforts frequently.

- Keep your letter to one page or less (around 300 words).

Types of Appreciation Letter:

There are 2 major types of appreciation letters. These are:

Personal Appreciation Letters and

Business Appreciation Letters.

Examples of personal appreciation letters include:

Appreciation letter to a friend

Appreciation letter to a neighbor, etc.

Examples of business appreciation letters:

Appreciation letter to a boss

Appreciation letter to an employee

Appreciation letter to a colleague

Appreciation letter to a team member

Retirement appreciation letter

Appreciation letter to the speaker of a seminar, etc.

Tips to Remember:

- For personal reasons, write a handwritten letter
- When writing to a firm's higher official, strive to utilize the corporate letterhead.
- Not flattery, but appreciation.
- Make sure the letter is proofread and edited for grammatical and spelling problems.
- Do not thank the person in advance.
- Be concise, but provide all pertinent facts. Don't just express gratitude for the day; express gratitude for assisting me with so and so task on that day. Again, don't express stuff like how worried you felt with aid from nowhere and how miserable you became as a result. Maintain the letter's focus on the recipient and his work, as well as the gratitude.

Merits of Gratitude letter:

Some psychology research suggests that writing such letters to show thanks can have emotional benefits, although this is not true in all cases. The custom of handwritten letters of gratitude has been reported in the news from a cultural standpoint, with some saying that the extra effort indicated by handwriting (as opposed to text messaging, for example) makes these letters more emotionally significant for both sender and recipient.

Gratitude Walk

A gratitude walk is a way of experiencing the world via your senses and thoughts as you meet it for the first time. It is pretty simple. Go outside and take a walk. Walk slowly, at a comfortable pace, it isn't about the destination for this, it truly is simply about the walking. Pay attention to what you see, hear, smell, and feel as you walk. Take note of where your attention is pulled, what you value, and the thoughts that come to mind. Get in touch with the feelings they elicit.

Extend any connections you make between these thoughts and feelings as you appreciate them. Experiment with your awareness's limitations. Consider what you're missing out on by not seeing, hearing, smelling, or feeling. The world is bigger than you and your perception of it. When you think about it, there's another thing to be thankful for. It implies that there is always something fresh to discover.

Where Do You Take Your Walks? And how long will it last?

It's acceptable to take a familiar walk—or venture down a path you've never travelled before. The journey is more important than the destination or even the way. This travel should take no more than 20 minutes, so don't feel compelled to keep checking the time on your phone. When it comes to phones, it's best to leave them at home, if at all possible. Sure, we're grateful for them, but they do have a tendency to draw our attention away from the rest of the world.

Investigate the Previously Unrecognized

You've looked into what you're not aware of. Now look for things you've never noticed before.

You've probably seen these trees a thousand times, but do you know what kind they are? Are you unsure? Make a mental note of their characteristics and set a reminder to find out more. Glance down where you normally look up. Take the turn at the corner where you always pass It's one thing to be thankful for life's blessings, the things we desire, work for, and obtain. But it's equally possible, and life-changing, to be grateful for the unexpected gifts we didn't ask for or expect. And for all of the delays and obstacles that appear to be getting in the way. It's possible that the travel is a metaphor for something.

Impacts of Gratitude walk:

Gratitude walk gives you powerful emotion. It not only feels wonderful in the moment, but it can also motivate you to achieve things.

Perhaps to repay your debt of appreciation, to take action in the direction of additional things to be grateful for, or simply to have a healthier and happier day today

Advantages
Physical
- Stronger immune systems
- Less bothered by aches and pains
- Lower blood pressure
- Exercise more and take better care of their health
- Sleep longer and feel more refreshed upon waking

Psychological:
- Higher levels of positive emotions
- More alert, alive, and awake
- More joy and pleasure
- More optimism and happiness

Social:

- More helpful, generous, and compassionate
- More forgiving
- More outgoing
- Feel less lonely and isolated.

Do you think you'll be up to trying a gratitude walk? You can do them with a friend, or like me alone enjoying God's beautiful creation. I wish you peace.

Daily Gratitude Journal

Something you've heard

1.
2.
3.
4.
5.

6.
7.
8.
9.
10.

Something you've seen

1.
2.
3.
4.
5.

6.
7.
8.
9.
10.

Something you've touched

1.
2.
3.
4.
5.

6.
7.
8.
9.
10.

Soothing and relaxing scents

1.
2.
3.
4.
5.

6.
7.
8.
9.
10.

Daily Gratitude Journal

Something you've felt

1.
2.
3.
4.
5.
6.
7.
8.
9.
10.

Something you've been given

1.
2.
3.
4.
5.
6.
7.
8.
9.
10.

Things that make you smile

1.
2.
3.
4.
5.
6.
7.
8.
9.
10.

What you've learned from falling?

1.
2.
3.
4.
5.
6.
7.
8.
9.
10.

Daily Gratitude Journal

People who've helped you up

1.
2.
3.
4.
5.
6.
7.
8.
9.
10.

Godly attributes

1.
2.
3.
4.
5.
6.
7.
8.
9.
10.

Words that inspire and motivate

1.
2.
3.
4.
5.
6.
7.
8.
9.
10.

Obstacles you've overcome

1.
2.
3.
4.
5.
6.
7.
8.
9.
10.

Daily Gratitude Journal

People who've taught and/or mentored you

1.
2.
3.
4.
5.
6.
7.
8.
9.
10.

The most beautiful things in nature

1.
2.
3.
4.
5.
6.
7.
8.
9.
10.

Favorite people/Best Friends

1.
2.
3.
4.
5.
6.
7.
8.
9.
10.

Notes

Daily Gratitude Journal

Date ___/___/___

Monday Tuesday Wednesday Thursday Friday Saturday Sunday

Scriptures, Quotes and Affirmations

_____
_____
_____
_____

What is the biggest obstacle you faced today?	What attributes, qualities were used to triumph?
_____	_____
_____	_____
_____	_____

Important takeaways about how you confronted the obstacles

_____
_____
_____
_____
_____

What I'm grateful for today?	Where is there room to grow?
_____	_____
_____	_____
_____	_____

Daily Gratitude Journal

Date ___/___/___

Monday Tuesday Wednesday Thursday Friday Saturday Sunday

Scriptures, Quotes and Affirmations

_____
_____
_____
_____
_____

What is the biggest obstacle you faced today?	What attributes, qualities were used to triumph?
_____	_____
_____	_____
_____	_____

Important takeaways about how you confronted the obstacles

_____
_____
_____
_____
_____

What I'm grateful for today?	Where is there room to grow?
_____	_____
_____	_____
_____	_____

Daily Gratitude Journal

Date ___/___/___

Monday Tuesday Wednesday Thursday Friday Saturday Sunday

Scriptures, Quotes and Affirmations

_____
_____
_____
_____
_____

What is the biggest obstacle you faced today?	What attributes, qualities were used to triumph?
_____	_____
_____	_____
_____	_____

Important takeaways about how you confronted the obstacles

_____
_____
_____
_____
_____

What I'm grateful for today?	Where is there room to grow?
_____	_____
_____	_____
_____	_____

Daily Gratitude Journal

Date ___/___/___

Monday   Tuesday   Wednesday   Thursday   Friday   Saturday   Sunday

Scriptures, Quotes and Affirmations

_____
_____
_____
_____
_____

What is the biggest obstacle you faced today?	What attributes, qualities were used to triumph?
_____	_____
_____	_____
_____	_____
_____	_____

Important takeaways about how you confronted the obstacles

_____
_____
_____
_____
_____

What I'm grateful for today?	Where is there room to grow?
_____	_____
_____	_____
_____	_____

Daily Gratitude Journal

Date ___/___/___

Monday Tuesday Wednesday Thursday Friday Saturday Sunday

Scriptures, Quotes and Affirmations

_____
_____
_____
_____
_____

What is the biggest obstacle you faced today?	What attributes, qualities were used to triumph?
_____	_____
_____	_____
_____	_____

Important takeaways about how you confronted the obstacles

_____
_____
_____
_____
_____
_____

What I'm grateful for today?	Where is there room to grow?
_____	_____
_____	_____
_____	_____

Daily Gratitude Journal

Date ___ / ___ / ___

Monday Tuesday Wednesday Thursday Friday Saturday Sunday

Scriptures, Quotes and Affirmations

_____
_____
_____
_____

What is the biggest obstacle you faced today?	What attributes, qualities were used to triumph?
_____	_____
_____	_____
_____	_____

Important takeaways about how you confronted the obstacles

_____
_____
_____
_____

What I'm grateful for today?	Where is there room to grow?
_____	_____
_____	_____
_____	_____

Daily Gratitude Journal

Date ___/___/___

Monday   Tuesday   Wednesday   Thursday   Friday   Saturday   Sunday

Scriptures, Quotes and Affirmations

_____
_____
_____
_____
_____

What is the biggest obstacle you faced today?	What attributes, qualities were used to triumph?
_____	_____
_____	_____
_____	_____
_____	_____

Important takeaways about how you confronted the obstacles

_____
_____
_____
_____
_____
_____

What I'm grateful for today?	Where is there room to grow?
_____	_____
_____	_____
_____	_____
_____	_____

Daily Gratitude Journal

Date ___/___/___

Monday   Tuesday   Wednesday   Thursday   Friday   Saturday   Sunday

Scriptures, Quotes and Affirmations

_____
_____
_____
_____

What is the biggest obstacle you faced today?	What attributes, qualities were used to triumph?
_____	_____
_____	_____
_____	_____

Important takeaways about how you confronted the obstacles

_____
_____
_____
_____

What I'm grateful for today?	Where is there room to grow?
_____	_____
_____	_____
_____	_____

Daily Gratitude Journal

Date ___/___/___

Monday   Tuesday   Wednesday   Thursday   Friday   Saturday   Sunday

Scriptures, Quotes and Affirmations

_____
_____
_____
_____

What is the biggest obstacle you faced today?	What attributes, qualities were used to triumph?
_____	_____
_____	_____
_____	_____
_____	_____

Important takeaways about how you confronted the obstacles

_____
_____
_____
_____
_____
_____

What I'm grateful for today?	Where is there room to grow?
_____	_____
_____	_____
_____	_____

Daily Gratitude Journal

Date ___/___/___

Monday Tuesday Wednesday Thursday Friday Saturday Sunday

Scriptures, Quotes and Affirmations

_____
_____
_____
_____
_____

What is the biggest obstacle you faced today?	What attributes, qualities were used to triumph?
_____	_____
_____	_____
_____	_____

Important takeaways about how you confronted the obstacles

_____
_____
_____
_____
_____

What I'm grateful for today?	Where is there room to grow?
_____	_____
_____	_____
_____	_____

Daily Gratitude Journal

Date ___/___/___

Monday Tuesday Wednesday Thursday Friday Saturday Sunday

Scriptures, Quotes and Affirmations

_____
_____
_____
_____
_____

What is the biggest obstacle you faced today?	What attributes, qualities were used to triumph?
_____	_____
_____	_____
_____	_____

Important takeaways about how you confronted the obstacles

_____
_____
_____
_____
_____

What I'm grateful for today?	Where is there room to grow?
_____	_____
_____	_____
_____	_____

Daily Gratitude Journal

Date ___ / ___ / ___

Monday Tuesday Wednesday Thursday Friday Saturday Sunday

Scriptures, Quotes and Affirmations

_____
_____
_____
_____

What is the biggest obstacle you faced today?	What attributes, qualities were used to triumph?
_____	_____
_____	_____
_____	_____

Important takeaways about how you confronted the obstacles

_____
_____
_____
_____
_____

What I'm grateful for today?	Where is there room to grow?
_____	_____
_____	_____
_____	_____

Daily Gratitude Journal

Date ___/___/___

Monday Tuesday Wednesday Thursday Friday Saturday Sunday

Scriptures, Quotes and Affirmations

_____
_____
_____
_____
_____

What is the biggest obstacle you faced today?	What attributes, qualities were used to triumph?
_____	_____
_____	_____
_____	_____

Important takeaways about how you confronted the obstacles

_____
_____
_____
_____
_____

What I'm grateful for today?	Where is there room to grow?
_____	_____
_____	_____
_____	_____

Daily Gratitude Journal

Date ___/___/___

Monday Tuesday Wednesday Thursday Friday Saturday Sunday

Scriptures, Quotes and Affirmations

_____
_____
_____
_____
_____

What is the biggest obstacle you faced today?	What attributes, qualities were used to triumph?
_____	_____
_____	_____
_____	_____

Important takeaways about how you confronted the obstacles

_____
_____
_____
_____
_____

What I'm grateful for today?	Where is there room to grow?
_____	_____
_____	_____
_____	_____

Daily Gratitude Journal

Date ___/___/___

Monday Tuesday Wednesday Thursday Friday Saturday Sunday

Scriptures, Quotes and Affirmations

_____
_____
_____
_____
_____

What is the biggest obstacle you faced today?	What attributes, qualities were used to triumph?
_____	_____
_____	_____
_____	_____
_____	_____

Important takeaways about how you confronted the obstacles

_____
_____
_____
_____
_____
_____

What I'm grateful for today?	Where is there room to grow?
_____	_____
_____	_____
_____	_____
_____	_____

Daily Gratitude Journal

Date ___/___/___

Monday   Tuesday   Wednesday   Thursday   Friday   Saturday   Sunday

Scriptures, Quotes and Affirmations

_____
_____
_____
_____

What is the biggest obstacle you faced today?	What attributes, qualities were used to triumph?
_____	_____
_____	_____
_____	_____

Important takeaways about how you confronted the obstacles

_____
_____
_____
_____
_____

What I'm grateful for today?	Where is there room to grow?
_____	_____
_____	_____
_____	_____

Daily Gratitude Journal

Date ___/___/___

Monday   Tuesday   Wednesday   Thursday   Friday   Saturday   Sunday

Scriptures, Quotes and Affirmations

_____
_____
_____
_____
_____

What is the biggest obstacle you faced today?	What attributes, qualities were used to triumph?
_____	_____
_____	_____
_____	_____
_____	_____

Important takeaways about how you confronted the obstacles

_____
_____
_____
_____
_____

What I'm grateful for today?	Where is there room to grow?
_____	_____
_____	_____
_____	_____

Daily Gratitude Journal

Date ___ / ___ / ___

Monday   Tuesday   Wednesday   Thursday   Friday   Saturday   Sunday

Scriptures, Quotes and Affirmations

_____
_____
_____
_____

What is the biggest obstacle you faced today?	What attributes, qualities were used to triumph?
_____	_____
_____	_____
_____	_____

Important takeaways about how you confronted the obstacles

_____
_____
_____
_____
_____

What I'm grateful for today?	Where is there room to grow?
_____	_____
_____	_____
_____	_____

Daily Gratitude Journal

Date ___/___/___

| Monday Tuesday Wednesday Thursday Friday Saturday Sunday |

Scriptures, Quotes and Affirmations

_____
_____
_____
_____

What is the biggest obstacle you faced today?	What attributes, qualities were used to triumph?
_____	_____
_____	_____
_____	_____
_____	_____

Important takeaways about how you confronted the obstacles

_____
_____
_____
_____
_____

What I'm grateful for today?	Where is there room to grow?
_____	_____
_____	_____
_____	_____
_____	_____

Daily Gratitude Journal

Date ___/___/___

Monday   Tuesday   Wednesday   Thursday   Friday   Saturday   Sunday

Scriptures, Quotes and Affirmations

_____
_____
_____
_____

What is the biggest obstacle you faced today?	What attributes, qualities were used to triumph?
_____	_____
_____	_____
_____	_____

Important takeaways about how you confronted the obstacles

_____
_____
_____
_____

What I'm grateful for today?	Where is there room to grow?
_____	_____
_____	_____
_____	_____

Daily Gratitude Journal

Date ___/___/___

Monday Tuesday Wednesday Thursday Friday Saturday Sunday

Scriptures, Quotes and Affirmations

_____
_____
_____
_____
_____

What is the biggest obstacle you faced today?	What attributes, qualities were used to triumph?
_____	_____
_____	_____
_____	_____
_____	_____

Important takeaways about how you confronted the obstacles

_____
_____
_____
_____
_____

What I'm grateful for today?	Where is there room to grow?
_____	_____
_____	_____
_____	_____
_____	_____

Daily Gratitude Journal

Date ___/___/___

Monday Tuesday Wednesday Thursday Friday Saturday Sunday

Scriptures, Quotes and Affirmations

_____
_____
_____
_____
_____

What is the biggest obstacle you faced today?	What attributes, qualities were used to triumph?
_____	_____
_____	_____
_____	_____
_____	_____

Important takeaways about how you confronted the obstacles

_____
_____
_____
_____
_____

What I'm grateful for today?	Where is there room to grow?
_____	_____
_____	_____
_____	_____

Daily Gratitude Journal

Date ___/___/___

Monday Tuesday Wednesday Thursday Friday Saturday Sunday

Scriptures, Quotes and Affirmations

_____
_____
_____
_____

What is the biggest obstacle you faced today?	What attributes, qualities were used to triumph?
_____	_____
_____	_____
_____	_____

Important takeaways about how you confronted the obstacles

_____
_____
_____
_____

What I'm grateful for today?	Where is there room to grow?
_____	_____
_____	_____
_____	_____

Daily Gratitude Journal

Date ___/___/___

Monday Tuesday Wednesday Thursday Friday Saturday Sunday

Scriptures, Quotes and Affirmations

_____
_____
_____
_____

What is the biggest obstacle you faced today?	What attributes, qualities were used to triumph?
_____	_____
_____	_____
_____	_____

Important takeaways about how you confronted the obstacles

_____
_____
_____
_____
_____

What I'm grateful for today?	Where is there room to grow?
_____	_____
_____	_____
_____	_____

Daily Gratitude Journal

Date ___/___/___

Monday   Tuesday   Wednesday   Thursday   Friday   Saturday   Sunday

Scriptures, Quotes and Affirmations

_____
_____
_____
_____

What is the biggest obstacle you faced today?	What attributes, qualities were used to triumph?
_____	_____
_____	_____
_____	_____

Important takeaways about how you confronted the obstacles

_____
_____
_____
_____

What I'm grateful for today?	Where is there room to grow?
_____	_____
_____	_____
_____	_____

Daily Gratitude Journal

Date ___/___/___

Monday   Tuesday   Wednesday   Thursday   Friday   Saturday   Sunday

Scriptures, Quotes and Affirmations

_____
_____
_____
_____

What is the biggest obstacle you faced today?	What attributes, qualities were used to triumph?
_____	_____
_____	_____
_____	_____
_____	_____

Important takeaways about how you confronted the obstacles

_____
_____
_____
_____
_____

What I'm grateful for today?	Where is there room to grow?
_____	_____
_____	_____
_____	_____

Daily Gratitude Journal

Date ___/___/___

Monday   Tuesday   Wednesday   Thursday   Friday   Saturday   Sunday

Scriptures, Quotes and Affirmations

_____
_____
_____
_____
_____

What is the biggest obstacle you faced today?	What attributes, qualities were used to triumph?
_____	_____
_____	_____
_____	_____
_____	_____

Important takeaways about how you confronted the obstacles

_____
_____
_____
_____
_____

What I'm grateful for today?	Where is there room to grow?
_____	_____
_____	_____
_____	_____

Daily Gratitude Journal

Date ___/___/___

Monday   Tuesday   Wednesday   Thursday   Friday   Saturday   Sunday

Scriptures, Quotes and Affirmations

_____
_____
_____
_____

What is the biggest obstacle you faced today?	What attributes, qualities were used to triumph?
_____	_____
_____	_____
_____	_____

Important takeaways about how you confronted the obstacles

_____
_____
_____
_____

What I'm grateful for today?	Where is there room to grow?
_____	_____
_____	_____
_____	_____

Daily Gratitude Journal

Date ___/___/___

Monday Tuesday Wednesday Thursday Friday Saturday Sunday

Scriptures, Quotes and Affirmations

_____
_____
_____
_____

What is the biggest obstacle you faced today?	What attributes, qualities were used to triumph?
_____	_____
_____	_____
_____	_____

Important takeaways about how you confronted the obstacles

_____
_____
_____
_____
_____

What I'm grateful for today?	Where is there room to grow?
_____	_____
_____	_____
_____	_____

Daily Gratitude Journal

Date ___/___/___

Monday Tuesday Wednesday Thursday Friday Saturday Sunday

Scriptures, Quotes and Affirmations

_____
_____
_____
_____

What is the biggest obstacle you faced today?	What attributes, qualities were used to triumph?
_____	_____
_____	_____
_____	_____

Important takeaways about how you confronted the obstacles

_____
_____
_____
_____
_____

What I'm grateful for today?	Where is there room to grow?
_____	_____
_____	_____
_____	_____

Daily Gratitude Journal

Date ___/___/___

Monday   Tuesday   Wednesday   Thursday   Friday   Saturday   Sunday

Scriptures, Quotes and Affirmations

_____
_____
_____
_____

What is the biggest obstacle you faced today?	What attributes, qualities were used to triumph?
_____	_____
_____	_____
_____	_____

Important takeaways about how you confronted the obstacles

_____
_____
_____
_____
_____
_____

What I'm grateful for today?	Where is there room to grow?
_____	_____
_____	_____
_____	_____

Daily Gratitude Journal

Date ___/___/___

Monday Tuesday Wednesday Thursday Friday Saturday Sunday

Scriptures, Quotes and Affirmations

_____
_____
_____
_____

What is the biggest obstacle you faced today?	What attributes, qualities were used to triumph?
_____	_____
_____	_____
_____	_____

Important takeaways about how you confronted the obstacles

_____
_____
_____
_____

What I'm grateful for today?	Where is there room to grow?
_____	_____
_____	_____
_____	_____

Daily Gratitude Journal

Date ___/___/___

Monday   Tuesday   Wednesday   Thursday   Friday   Saturday   Sunday

Scriptures, Quotes and Affirmations

_____
_____
_____
_____

What is the biggest obstacle you faced today?	What attributes, qualities were used to triumph?
_____	_____
_____	_____
_____	_____

Important takeaways about how you confronted the obstacles

_____
_____
_____
_____
_____

What I'm grateful for today?	Where is there room to grow?
_____	_____
_____	_____
_____	_____

Daily Gratitude Journal

Date ___/___/___

Monday   Tuesday   Wednesday   Thursday   Friday   Saturday   Sunday

Scriptures, Quotes and Affirmations

_____
_____
_____
_____
_____

What is the biggest obstacle you faced today?	What attributes, qualities were used to triumph?
_____	_____
_____	_____
_____	_____

Important takeaways about how you confronted the obstacles

_____
_____
_____
_____
_____

What I'm grateful for today?	Where is there room to grow?
_____	_____
_____	_____
_____	_____

Daily Gratitude Journal

Date ___/___/___

Monday   Tuesday   Wednesday   Thursday   Friday   Saturday   Sunday

Scriptures, Quotes and Affirmations

_____
_____
_____
_____

What is the biggest obstacle you faced today?	What attributes, qualities were used to triumph?
_____	_____
_____	_____
_____	_____

Important takeaways about how you confronted the obstacles

_____
_____
_____
_____
_____

What I'm grateful for today?	Where is there room to grow?
_____	_____
_____	_____
_____	_____

Daily Gratitude Journal

Date ___/___/___

Monday Tuesday Wednesday Thursday Friday Saturday Sunday

Scriptures, Quotes and Affirmations

_____
_____
_____
_____

What is the biggest obstacle you faced today?	What attributes, qualities were used to triumph?
_____	_____
_____	_____
_____	_____

Important takeaways about how you confronted the obstacles

_____
_____
_____
_____

What I'm grateful for today?	Where is there room to grow?
_____	_____
_____	_____
_____	_____

Daily Gratitude Journal

Date ___/___/___

Monday Tuesday Wednesday Thursday Friday Saturday Sunday

Scriptures, Quotes and Affirmations

_____
_____
_____
_____

What is the biggest obstacle you faced today?	What attributes, qualities were used to triumph?
_____	_____
_____	_____
_____	_____
_____	_____

Important takeaways about how you confronted the obstacles

_____
_____
_____
_____
_____

What I'm grateful for today?	Where is there room to grow?
_____	_____
_____	_____
_____	_____
_____	_____

Daily Gratitude Journal

Date ___/___/___

Monday   Tuesday   Wednesday   Thursday   Friday   Saturday   Sunday

Scriptures, Quotes and Affirmations

_____
_____
_____
_____

What is the biggest obstacle you faced today?	What attributes, qualities were used to triumph?
_____	_____
_____	_____
_____	_____

Important takeaways about how you confronted the obstacles

_____
_____
_____
_____

What I'm grateful for today?	Where is there room to grow?
_____	_____
_____	_____
_____	_____

Daily Gratitude Journal

Date ___/___/___

Monday   Tuesday   Wednesday   Thursday   Friday   Saturday   Sunday

Scriptures, Quotes and Affirmations

_____
_____
_____
_____
_____

What is the biggest obstacle you faced today?	What attributes, qualities were used to triumph?
_____	_____
_____	_____
_____	_____
_____	_____

Important takeaways about how you confronted the obstacles

_____
_____
_____
_____
_____

What I'm grateful for today?	Where is there room to grow?
_____	_____
_____	_____
_____	_____

Daily Gratitude Journal

Date ___/___/___

Monday   Tuesday   Wednesday   Thursday   Friday   Saturday   Sunday

Scriptures, Quotes and Affirmations

_____
_____
_____
_____

What is the biggest obstacle you faced today?	What attributes, qualities were used to triumph?
_____	_____
_____	_____
_____	_____

Important takeaways about how you confronted the obstacles

_____
_____
_____
_____

What I'm grateful for today?	Where is there room to grow?
_____	_____
_____	_____
_____	_____

Daily Gratitude Journal

Date ___/___/___

Monday Tuesday Wednesday Thursday Friday Saturday Sunday

Scriptures, Quotes and Affirmations

_____
_____
_____
_____
_____

What is the biggest obstacle you faced today?	What attributes, qualities were used to triumph?
_____	_____
_____	_____
_____	_____
_____	_____

Important takeaways about how you confronted the obstacles

_____
_____
_____
_____
_____

What I'm grateful for today?	Where is there room to grow?
_____	_____
_____	_____
_____	_____

Daily Gratitude Journal

Date ___ / ___ / ___

Monday   Tuesday   Wednesday   Thursday   Friday   Saturday   Sunday

Scriptures, Quotes and Affirmations

_____
_____
_____
_____

What is the biggest obstacle you faced today?	What attributes, qualities were used to triumph?
_____	_____
_____	_____
_____	_____

Important takeaways about how you confronted the obstacles

_____
_____
_____
_____
_____

What I'm grateful for today?	Where is there room to grow?
_____	_____
_____	_____
_____	_____

Daily Gratitude Journal

Date ___/___/___

Monday Tuesday Wednesday Thursday Friday Saturday Sunday

Scriptures, Quotes and Affirmations

_____
_____
_____
_____

What is the biggest obstacle you faced today?	What attributes, qualities were used to triumph?
_____	_____
_____	_____
_____	_____

Important takeaways about how you confronted the obstacles

_____
_____
_____
_____
_____
_____

What I'm grateful for today?	Where is there room to grow?
_____	_____
_____	_____
_____	_____

Daily Gratitude Journal

Date ___/___/___

Monday Tuesday Wednesday Thursday Friday Saturday Sunday

Scriptures, Quotes and Affirmations

_____
_____
_____
_____

What is the biggest obstacle you faced today?	What attributes, qualities were used to triumph?
_____	_____
_____	_____
_____	_____

Important takeaways about how you confronted the obstacles

_____
_____
_____
_____
_____

What I'm grateful for today?	Where is there room to grow?
_____	_____
_____	_____
_____	_____

Daily Gratitude Journal

Date ___/___/___

Monday Tuesday Wednesday Thursday Friday Saturday Sunday

Scriptures, Quotes and Affirmations

_____
_____
_____
_____

What is the biggest obstacle you faced today?	What attributes, qualities were used to triumph?
_____	_____
_____	_____
_____	_____

Important takeaways about how you confronted the obstacles

_____
_____
_____
_____

What I'm grateful for today?	Where is there room to grow?
_____	_____
_____	_____
_____	_____

Daily Gratitude Journal

Date ___/___/___

Monday Tuesday Wednesday Thursday Friday Saturday Sunday

Scriptures, Quotes and Affirmations

_____
_____
_____
_____

What is the biggest obstacle you faced today?	What attributes, qualities were used to triumph?
_____	_____
_____	_____
_____	_____

Important takeaways about how you confronted the obstacles

_____
_____
_____
_____

What I'm grateful for today?	Where is there room to grow?
_____	_____
_____	_____
_____	_____

Daily Gratitude Journal

Date ___/___/___

Monday   Tuesday   Wednesday   Thursday   Friday   Saturday   Sunday

Scriptures, Quotes and Affirmations

_____
_____
_____
_____

What is the biggest obstacle you faced today?	What attributes, qualities were used to triumph?
_____	_____
_____	_____
_____	_____
_____	_____

Important takeaways about how you confronted the obstacles

_____
_____
_____
_____
_____

What I'm grateful for today?	Where is there room to grow?
_____	_____
_____	_____
_____	_____

Daily Gratitude Journal

Date ___/___/___

Monday Tuesday Wednesday Thursday Friday Saturday Sunday

Scriptures, Quotes and Affirmations

_____
_____
_____
_____

What is the biggest obstacle you faced today?	What attributes, qualities were used to triumph?
_____	_____
_____	_____
_____	_____

Important takeaways about how you confronted the obstacles

_____
_____
_____
_____
_____

What I'm grateful for today?	Where is there room to grow?
_____	_____
_____	_____
_____	_____

Daily Gratitude Journal

Date ___/___/___

Monday Tuesday Wednesday Thursday Friday Saturday Sunday

Scriptures, Quotes and Affirmations

_____
_____
_____
_____
_____

What is the biggest obstacle you faced today?	What attributes, qualities were used to triumph?
_____	_____
_____	_____
_____	_____

Important takeaways about how you confronted the obstacles

_____
_____
_____
_____
_____
_____

What I'm grateful for today?	Where is there room to grow?
_____	_____
_____	_____
_____	_____

Daily Gratitude Journal

Date ___/___/___

Monday   Tuesday   Wednesday   Thursday   Friday   Saturday   Sunday

Scriptures, Quotes and Affirmations

_____
_____
_____
_____

What is the biggest obstacle you faced today?	What attributes, qualities were used to triumph?
_____	_____
_____	_____
_____	_____

Important takeaways about how you confronted the obstacles

_____
_____
_____
_____

What I'm grateful for today?	Where is there room to grow?
_____	_____
_____	_____
_____	_____

Daily Gratitude Journal

Date ___/___/___

Monday Tuesday Wednesday Thursday Friday Saturday Sunday

Scriptures, Quotes and Affirmations

_____
_____
_____
_____
_____

What is the biggest obstacle you faced today?	What attributes, qualities were used to triumph?
_____	_____
_____	_____
_____	_____
_____	_____

Important takeaways about how you confronted the obstacles

_____
_____
_____
_____
_____

What I'm grateful for today?	Where is there room to grow?
_____	_____
_____	_____
_____	_____
_____	_____

Daily Gratitude Journal

Date ___/___/___

Monday   Tuesday   Wednesday   Thursday   Friday   Saturday   Sunday

Scriptures, Quotes and Affirmations

_____
_____
_____
_____

What is the biggest obstacle you faced today?	What attributes, qualities were used to triumph?
_____	_____
_____	_____
_____	_____

Important takeaways about how you confronted the obstacles

_____
_____
_____
_____

What I'm grateful for today?	Where is there room to grow?
_____	_____
_____	_____
_____	_____

Daily Gratitude Journal

Date ___/___/___

Monday Tuesday Wednesday Thursday Friday Saturday Sunday

Scriptures, Quotes and Affirmations

_____
_____
_____
_____

What is the biggest obstacle you faced today?	What attributes, qualities were used to triumph?
_____	_____
_____	_____
_____	_____

Important takeaways about how you confronted the obstacles

_____
_____
_____
_____

What I'm grateful for today?	Where is there room to grow?
_____	_____
_____	_____
_____	_____

Daily Gratitude Journal

Date ___ / ___ / ___

Monday   Tuesday   Wednesday   Thursday   Friday   Saturday   Sunday

Scriptures, Quotes and Affirmations

_____
_____
_____
_____

What is the biggest obstacle you faced today?

_____
_____
_____

What attributes, qualities were used to triumph?

_____
_____
_____

Important takeaways about how you confronted the obstacles

_____
_____
_____
_____
_____

What I'm grateful for today?

_____
_____
_____

Where is there room to grow?

_____
_____
_____

Daily Gratitude Journal

Date ___ / ___ / ___

Monday Tuesday Wednesday Thursday Friday Saturday Sunday

Scriptures, Quotes and Affirmations

_____
_____
_____
_____

What is the biggest obstacle you faced today?	What attributes, qualities were used to triumph?
_____	_____
_____	_____
_____	_____
_____	_____

Important takeaways about how you confronted the obstacles

_____
_____
_____
_____
_____

What I'm grateful for today?	Where is there room to grow?
_____	_____
_____	_____
_____	_____

Daily Gratitude Journal

Date ___/___/___

Monday Tuesday Wednesday Thursday Friday Saturday Sunday

Scriptures, Quotes and Affirmations

_____
_____
_____
_____
_____

What is the biggest obstacle you faced today?	What attributes, qualities were used to triumph?
_____	_____
_____	_____
_____	_____

Important takeaways about how you confronted the obstacles

_____
_____
_____
_____
_____

What I'm grateful for today?	Where is there room to grow?
_____	_____
_____	_____
_____	_____

Daily Gratitude Journal

Date ___/___/___

Monday   Tuesday   Wednesday   Thursday   Friday   Saturday   Sunday

Scriptures, Quotes and Affirmations

_____
_____
_____
_____

What is the biggest obstacle you faced today?	What attributes, qualities were used to triumph?
_____	_____
_____	_____
_____	_____
_____	_____

Important takeaways about how you confronted the obstacles

_____
_____
_____
_____
_____

What I'm grateful for today?	Where is there room to grow?
_____	_____
_____	_____
_____	_____

Daily Gratitude Journal

Date ___/___/___

Monday   Tuesday   Wednesday   Thursday   Friday   Saturday   Sunday

Scriptures, Quotes and Affirmations

_____
_____
_____
_____
_____

What is the biggest obstacle you faced today?	What attributes, qualities were used to triumph?
_____	_____
_____	_____
_____	_____

Important takeaways about how you confronted the obstacles

_____
_____
_____
_____
_____

What I'm grateful for today?	Where is there room to grow?
_____	_____
_____	_____
_____	_____

Daily Gratitude Journal

Date ___/___/___

Monday   Tuesday   Wednesday   Thursday   Friday   Saturday   Sunday

Scriptures, Quotes and Affirmations

_____
_____
_____
_____

What is the biggest obstacle you faced today?	What attributes, qualities were used to triumph?
_____	_____
_____	_____
_____	_____

Important takeaways about how you confronted the obstacles

_____
_____
_____
_____

What I'm grateful for today?	Where is there room to grow?
_____	_____
_____	_____
_____	_____

Daily Gratitude Journal

Date ___/___/___

Monday Tuesday Wednesday Thursday Friday Saturday Sunday

Scriptures, Quotes and Affirmations

_____
_____
_____
_____

What is the biggest obstacle you faced today?

What attributes, qualities were used to triumph?

Important takeaways about how you confronted the obstacles

_____
_____
_____
_____
_____

What I'm grateful for today?

Where is there room to grow?

Daily Gratitude Journal

Date ___ / ___ / ___

Monday Tuesday Wednesday Thursday Friday Saturday Sunday

Scriptures, Quotes and Affirmations

_____
_____
_____
_____

What is the biggest obstacle you faced today?	What attributes, qualities were used to triumph?
_____	_____
_____	_____
_____	_____
_____	_____

Important takeaways about how you confronted the obstacles

_____
_____
_____
_____
_____

What I'm grateful for today?	Where is there room to grow?
_____	_____
_____	_____
_____	_____
_____	_____

Daily Gratitude Journal

Date ___ / ___ / ___

Monday Tuesday Wednesday Thursday Friday Saturday Sunday

Scriptures, Quotes and Affirmations

_____
_____
_____
_____

What is the biggest obstacle you faced today?	What attributes, qualities were used to triumph?
_____	_____
_____	_____
_____	_____
_____	_____

Important takeaways about how you confronted the obstacles

_____
_____
_____
_____
_____

What I'm grateful for today?	Where is there room to grow?
_____	_____
_____	_____
_____	_____
_____	_____

Daily Gratitude Journal

Date ___/___/___

Monday Tuesday Wednesday Thursday Friday Saturday Sunday

Scriptures, Quotes and Affirmations

_____
_____
_____
_____

What is the biggest obstacle you faced today?

What attributes, qualities were used to triumph?

_____
_____
_____
_____

Important takeaways about how you confronted the obstacles

_____
_____
_____
_____
_____

What I'm grateful for today?

Where is there room to grow?

_____
_____
_____

Daily Gratitude Journal

Date ___/___/___

Monday Tuesday Wednesday Thursday Friday Saturday Sunday

Scriptures, Quotes and Affirmations

_____
_____
_____
_____

What is the biggest obstacle you faced today?	What attributes, qualities were used to triumph?
_____	_____
_____	_____
_____	_____
_____	_____

Important takeaways about how you confronted the obstacles

_____
_____
_____
_____
_____

What I'm grateful for today?	Where is there room to grow?
_____	_____
_____	_____
_____	_____

Daily Gratitude Journal

Date ___/___/___

Monday Tuesday Wednesday Thursday Friday Saturday Sunday

Scriptures, Quotes and Affirmations

_____
_____
_____
_____

What is the biggest obstacle you faced today?	What attributes, qualities were used to triumph?
_____	_____
_____	_____
_____	_____
_____	_____

Important takeaways about how you confronted the obstacles

_____
_____
_____
_____
_____
_____

What I'm grateful for today?	Where is there room to grow?
_____	_____
_____	_____
_____	_____

Daily Gratitude Journal

Date ___/___/___

Monday   Tuesday   Wednesday   Thursday   Friday   Saturday   Sunday

Scriptures, Quotes and Affirmations

_____
_____
_____
_____

What is the biggest obstacle you faced today?	What attributes, qualities were used to triumph?
_____	_____
_____	_____
_____	_____
_____	_____

Important takeaways about how you confronted the obstacles

_____
_____
_____
_____
_____

What I'm grateful for today?	Where is there room to grow?
_____	_____
_____	_____
_____	_____

Daily Gratitude Journal

Date ___/___/___

Monday Tuesday Wednesday Thursday Friday Saturday Sunday

Scriptures, Quotes and Affirmations

_____
_____
_____
_____
_____

What is the biggest obstacle you faced today?	What attributes, qualities were used to triumph?
_____	_____
_____	_____
_____	_____
_____	_____

Important takeaways about how you confronted the obstacles

_____
_____
_____
_____
_____

What I'm grateful for today?	Where is there room to grow?
_____	_____
_____	_____
_____	_____

Daily Gratitude Journal

Date ___/___/___

Monday   Tuesday   Wednesday   Thursday   Friday   Saturday   Sunday

Scriptures, Quotes and Affirmations

_____
_____
_____
_____
_____

What is the biggest obstacle you faced today?	What attributes, qualities were used to triumph?
_____	_____
_____	_____
_____	_____
_____	_____

Important takeaways about how you confronted the obstacles

_____
_____
_____
_____
_____
_____

What I'm grateful for today?	Where is there room to grow?
_____	_____
_____	_____
_____	_____

Daily Gratitude Journal

Date ___/___/___

Monday   Tuesday   Wednesday   Thursday   Friday   Saturday   Sunday

Scriptures, Quotes and Affirmations

_____
_____
_____
_____

What is the biggest obstacle you faced today?	What attributes, qualities were used to triumph?
_____	_____
_____	_____
_____	_____

Important takeaways about how you confronted the obstacles

_____
_____
_____
_____
_____
_____

What I'm grateful for today?	Where is there room to grow?
_____	_____
_____	_____
_____	_____

Daily Gratitude Journal

Date ___/___/___

Monday   Tuesday   Wednesday   Thursday   Friday   Saturday   Sunday

Scriptures, Quotes and Affirmations

_____
_____
_____
_____

What is the biggest obstacle you faced today?	What attributes, qualities were used to triumph?
_____	_____
_____	_____
_____	_____
_____	_____

Important takeaways about how you confronted the obstacles

_____
_____
_____
_____
_____

What I'm grateful for today?	Where is there room to grow?
_____	_____
_____	_____
_____	_____

Daily Gratitude Journal

Date ___/___/___

Monday Tuesday Wednesday Thursday Friday Saturday Sunday

Scriptures, Quotes and Affirmations

_____
_____
_____
_____

What is the biggest obstacle you faced today?	What attributes, qualities were used to triumph?
_____	_____
_____	_____
_____	_____
_____	_____

Important takeaways about how you confronted the obstacles

_____
_____
_____
_____
_____

What I'm grateful for today?	Where is there room to grow?
_____	_____
_____	_____
_____	_____

Daily Gratitude Journal

Date ___/___/___

Monday Tuesday Wednesday Thursday Friday Saturday Sunday

Scriptures, Quotes and Affirmations

_____
_____
_____
_____

What is the biggest obstacle you faced today?	What attributes, qualities were used to triumph?
_____	_____
_____	_____
_____	_____

Important takeaways about how you confronted the obstacles

_____
_____
_____
_____
_____

What I'm grateful for today?	Where is there room to grow?
_____	_____
_____	_____
_____	_____

Daily Gratitude Journal

Date ___/___/___

Monday   Tuesday   Wednesday   Thursday   Friday   Saturday   Sunday

Scriptures, Quotes and Affirmations

_____
_____
_____
_____
_____

What is the biggest obstacle you faced today?	What attributes, qualities were used to triumph?
_____	_____
_____	_____
_____	_____
_____	_____

Important takeaways about how you confronted the obstacles

_____
_____
_____
_____
_____

What I'm grateful for today?	Where is there room to grow?
_____	_____
_____	_____
_____	_____

Daily Gratitude Journal

Date ___/___/___

Monday   Tuesday   Wednesday   Thursday   Friday   Saturday   Sunday

Scriptures, Quotes and Affirmations

_____
_____
_____
_____

What is the biggest obstacle you faced today?	What attributes, qualities were used to triumph?

Important takeaways about how you confronted the obstacles

_____
_____
_____
_____
_____

What I'm grateful for today?	Where is there room to grow?

Daily Gratitude Journal

Date ___/___/___

Monday Tuesday Wednesday Thursday Friday Saturday Sunday

Scriptures, Quotes and Affirmations

_____
_____
_____
_____
_____

What is the biggest obstacle you faced today?	What attributes, qualities were used to triumph?
_____	_____
_____	_____
_____	_____
_____	_____

Important takeaways about how you confronted the obstacles

_____
_____
_____
_____
_____
_____

What I'm grateful for today?	Where is there room to grow?
_____	_____
_____	_____
_____	_____

Daily Gratitude Journal

Date ___/___/___

Monday   Tuesday   Wednesday   Thursday   Friday   Saturday   Sunday

Scriptures, Quotes and Affirmations

_____
_____
_____
_____

What is the biggest obstacle you faced today?	What attributes, qualities were used to triumph?
_____	_____
_____	_____
_____	_____
_____	_____

Important takeaways about how you confronted the obstacles

_____
_____
_____
_____
_____

What I'm grateful for today?	Where is there room to grow?
_____	_____
_____	_____
_____	_____

Daily Gratitude Journal

Date ___/___/___

Monday Tuesday Wednesday Thursday Friday Saturday Sunday

Scriptures, Quotes and Affirmations

_____
_____
_____
_____

What is the biggest obstacle you faced today?	What attributes, qualities were used to triumph?
_____	_____
_____	_____
_____	_____

Important takeaways about how you confronted the obstacles

_____
_____
_____
_____
_____

What I'm grateful for today?	Where is there room to grow?
_____	_____
_____	_____
_____	_____

Daily Gratitude Journal

Date ___/___/___

Monday Tuesday Wednesday Thursday Friday Saturday Sunday

Scriptures, Quotes and Affirmations

_____
_____
_____
_____

What is the biggest obstacle you faced today?	What attributes, qualities were used to triumph?
_____	_____
_____	_____
_____	_____
_____	_____

Important takeaways about how you confronted the obstacles

_____
_____
_____
_____

What I'm grateful for today?	Where is there room to grow?
_____	_____
_____	_____
_____	_____

Daily Gratitude Journal

Date ___/___/___

Monday   Tuesday   Wednesday   Thursday   Friday   Saturday   Sunday

Scriptures, Quotes and Affirmations

_____
_____
_____
_____
_____

What is the biggest obstacle you faced today?	What attributes, qualities were used to triumph?
_____	_____
_____	_____
_____	_____
_____	_____

Important takeaways about how you confronted the obstacles

_____
_____
_____
_____
_____

What I'm grateful for today?	Where is there room to grow?
_____	_____
_____	_____
_____	_____

Daily Gratitude Journal

Date ___/___/___

Monday   Tuesday   Wednesday   Thursday   Friday   Saturday   Sunday

Scriptures, Quotes and Affirmations

_____
_____
_____
_____
_____

What is the biggest obstacle you faced today?	What attributes, qualities were used to triumph?
_____	_____
_____	_____
_____	_____
_____	_____

Important takeaways about how you confronted the obstacles

_____
_____
_____
_____
_____
_____

What I'm grateful for today?	Where is there room to grow?
_____	_____
_____	_____
_____	_____

Daily Gratitude Journal

Date ___/___/___

Monday Tuesday Wednesday Thursday Friday Saturday Sunday

Scriptures, Quotes and Affirmations

_____
_____
_____
_____

What is the biggest obstacle you faced today?	What attributes, qualities were used to triumph?
_____	_____
_____	_____
_____	_____
_____	_____

Important takeaways about how you confronted the obstacles

_____
_____
_____
_____
_____

What I'm grateful for today?	Where is there room to grow?
_____	_____
_____	_____
_____	_____

Daily Gratitude Journal

Date ___/___/___

Monday   Tuesday   Wednesday   Thursday   Friday   Saturday   Sunday

Scriptures, Quotes and Affirmations

_____
_____
_____
_____
_____

What is the biggest obstacle you faced today?	What attributes, qualities were used to triumph?
_____	_____
_____	_____
_____	_____

Important takeaways about how you confronted the obstacles

_____
_____
_____
_____
_____

What I'm grateful for today?	Where is there room to grow?
_____	_____
_____	_____
_____	_____

Daily Gratitude Journal

Date ___/___/___

Monday Tuesday Wednesday Thursday Friday Saturday Sunday

Scriptures, Quotes and Affirmations

_____
_____
_____
_____
_____

What is the biggest obstacle you faced today?	What attributes, qualities were used to triumph?
_____	_____
_____	_____
_____	_____

Important takeaways about how you confronted the obstacles

_____
_____
_____
_____
_____

What I'm grateful for today?	Where is there room to grow?
_____	_____
_____	_____
_____	_____

Daily Gratitude Journal

Date ___/___/___

Monday Tuesday Wednesday Thursday Friday Saturday Sunday

Scriptures, Quotes and Affirmations

_____
_____
_____
_____

What is the biggest obstacle you faced today?	What attributes, qualities were used to triumph?

Important takeaways about how you confronted the obstacles

_____
_____
_____
_____

What I'm grateful for today?	Where is there room to grow?

Daily Gratitude Journal

Date ___/___/___

Monday Tuesday Wednesday Thursday Friday Saturday Sunday

Scriptures, Quotes and Affirmations

_____
_____
_____
_____
_____

What is the biggest obstacle you faced today?	What attributes, qualities were used to triumph?
_____	_____
_____	_____
_____	_____
_____	_____

Important takeaways about how you confronted the obstacles

_____
_____
_____
_____
_____
_____

What I'm grateful for today?	Where is there room to grow?
_____	_____
_____	_____
_____	_____
_____	_____

Daily Gratitude Journal

Date ___/___/___

Monday Tuesday Wednesday Thursday Friday Saturday Sunday

Scriptures, Quotes and Affirmations

_____
_____
_____
_____
_____

What is the biggest obstacle you faced today?	What attributes, qualities were used to triumph?
_____	_____
_____	_____
_____	_____
_____	_____

Important takeaways about how you confronted the obstacles

_____
_____
_____
_____
_____

What I'm grateful for today?	Where is there room to grow?
_____	_____
_____	_____
_____	_____

Daily Gratitude Journal

Date ___/___/___

Monday Tuesday Wednesday Thursday Friday Saturday Sunday

Scriptures, Quotes and Affirmations

_____
_____
_____
_____

What is the biggest obstacle you faced today?	What attributes, qualities were used to triumph?

Important takeaways about how you confronted the obstacles

_____
_____
_____
_____

What I'm grateful for today?	Where is there room to grow?

Daily Gratitude Journal

Date ___/___/___

Monday Tuesday Wednesday Thursday Friday Saturday Sunday

Scriptures, Quotes and Affirmations

_____
_____
_____
_____

What is the biggest obstacle you faced today?	What attributes, qualities were used to triumph?

Important takeaways about how you confronted the obstacles

_____
_____
_____
_____
_____

What I'm grateful for today?	Where is there room to grow?

Daily Gratitude Journal

Date ___/___/___

Monday   Tuesday   Wednesday   Thursday   Friday   Saturday   Sunday

Scriptures, Quotes and Affirmations

_____
_____
_____
_____
_____

What is the biggest obstacle you faced today?	What attributes, qualities were used to triumph?
_____	_____
_____	_____
_____	_____

Important takeaways about how you confronted the obstacles

_____
_____
_____
_____
_____

What I'm grateful for today?	Where is there room to grow?
_____	_____
_____	_____
_____	_____

Publication Information

Website: soundhealingwithmj.com
Mailing Address: 539 W Commerce St, Suite 847, Dallas Tx, 75208

Copyright 2021 The Griot Journal. All rights reserved

No part of this publication may be reproduced, distributed or transmitted, in any form or by any means, including photocopying, recording or other electronic or mechanical methods, without the prior written permission of the publisher, except in the case of brief quotations embodied in reviews and certain other non commercial uses permitted by copyright law.

ISBN: 978-1-956488-01-2

www.ingramcontent.com/pod-product-compliance
Lightning Source LLC
Chambersburg PA
CBHW070553160426
43199CB00014B/2481